MAY 11 '98

DAVE BING

Basketball Great with a Heart

DAVE BING

Basketball Great with a Heart

Elizabeth Schleichert

—Multicultural Junior Biographies—

ENSLOW PUBLISHERS, INC.

44 Fadem Rd.	P.O. Box 38
Box 699	Aldershot
Springfield, N.J. 07081	Hants GU12 6BP
U.S.A.	U.K.

Library of Congress Cataloging-in-Publication Data

Schleichert, Elizabeth.
    Dave Bing: Basketball Great With a Heart/Elizabeth Schleichert
        p. cm. — (Multicultural Junior Biographies)
    Includes bibliographical references (p.) and index.
    ISBN 0-89490-635-6
    1. Bing, Dave, 1943– —Juvenile literature. 2. Basketball players—United
States—Biography—Juvenile literature. 3. Detroit Pistons (Basketball team)—
Juvenile literature. [1. Bing, Dave, 1943– . 2. Basketball players. 3. Detroit
Pistons (Basketball team) 4. Afro-Americans—Biography.] I. Title. II. Series.
GV884.B56S35   1995
796.323'092—dc20
    [B]   94-43562
                                                                    CIP
                                                                    AC

Printed in the United States of America

10 9 8 7 6 5 4 3 2 1

Illustration Credits: Courtesy of Dave Bing, pp. 10, 18, 25, 34, 46, 48, 53, 55, 58, 60,
67, 69, 74, 77 ; Detroit Pistons, pp. 12, 40; Einstein Photos, p. 42.

Cover Illustration: Courtesy of Dave Bing.

CONTENTS

THE BIG GAME

It was November 18, 1966—still early in the professional basketball season. Just five thousand fans had come to Cobo Arena in Detroit, Michigan, to see the Pistons play the Los Angeles Lakers. The arena was only half full because the Detroit Pistons had been playing poorly for the last ten years. Only true fans had turned out for this game. Before long, members of the home team, wearing their bright blue uniforms, jogged onto the court. One of the players wore number 21. He was a thin guard named Dave Bing. He had just joined the Pistons that season. So far, no one knew much about him. In fact, in the last game, Bing had not scored a single point. There was no reason to think that this night would be any different.

Starting in the Big Game

Dave Bing was in the starting lineup that night. As soon as the ball got moving, so did Bing. He kept stealing the ball from the Lakers players. Every time the ball bounced off the backboard, he rebounded it. Once Bing had the ball, he quickly danced and dodged his way downcourt. He seemed unstoppable. He kept leaping above the players on the other team. He kept scoring. He had 35 points that night. The fans kept standing up to cheer for Dave Bing. Some of them never sat down at all! It was a great game.

In the middle of the game, Dave Bing jumped up over Laker player Marvin "Bad News" Barnes. Barnes somehow knocked Bing to the floor. He lay there without moving for what seemed like forever. After a few minutes, he rolled over and slowly stood. He shook his head trying to lose the dazed feeling. Then he ran back to join his teammates. The crowd rose and chanted "Bing! Bing! Bing!"

Thanks to Dave Bing the Pistons beat the

Lakers that night, 121–118. Dave Bing had become a hero to Pistons fans.[1]

Becoming a Star

By the following season, Dave Bing was a well-known star in the National Basketball Association (NBA).[2] He would play basketball for twelve years. For nine of those years, he would be with the Detroit Pistons. He also played briefly with the Washington Bullets and Boston Celtics. He is one of only four players in NBA history to be in the top 20 in both scoring and assists in his career.[3] (An assist is a pass that enables a teammate to score.) Dave Bing played on seven All-Star teams.[4] In 1990 he received the sport's highest honor. He was elected to the Basketball Hall of Fame.[5]

Basketball and More

Dave Bing's winning basketball career is only part of his story. Today, Dave Bing is more than just a sports legend. Many athletes make no plans for life after sports. They may advertise sports shoes on television. Or, they may open a

Dave Bing played a brief part of his professional basketball career with the Boston Celtics. In this game at the Boston Garden, Bing is positioning himself against his Cleveland Cavaliers opponent.

business. But often they hire someone else to run their new business. Sometimes the person they hire doesn't do the job well. Former athletes have found themselves with no money. There are many stories of athletes who have lost the millions of dollars they once earned playing sports. They didn't know what to do when their sports careers were over.[6]

Dave Bing isn't one of these athletes. He is now a very successful businessman in Detroit. Over the last ten years or so, he has used the traits that made him a success on the basketball court. He has started his own companies. Dave Bing is now one of the top minority business owners in the country. His companies employ more than two hundred people. Recent yearly sales from all of his companies were more than $75 million.[7]

How has Bing done all this? What is he all about, and where did he come from? How has he been able to succeed where so many have failed? What has he done to help others?

Dave Bing has never stopped setting new goals for himself. He is always making new plans. He keeps pushing himself. But he has never forgotten his roots. He has never stopped trying

*Dave Bing's winning basketball career is an exciting part of his life.
It is however, only a part of his life. He has taken many of the skills
and talents he used on the court into the world of busineess.*

to help those who are less fortunate than he is. He has done a lot for young African Americans. He now has the respect of both Detroit's business leaders and its citizens — black and white.[8]

He once said:

"It's important to me to have success. But I'm not so driven to make money that I forget what my community [the African-American one] is going through right now. I want to succeed so I can be a good role model and have a positive impact on my community. I want to help people and let them know that somebody cares about them."[9]

He is determined to be the best that he can be. He is also giving back what he has learned along the way. Dave Bing is a winner no matter how you look at it.

THE EARLY YEARS

On November 29, 1943, Juanita and Hasker Bing's second child, David, was born. He was their first son. He had an older sister, Dorothy. The Bing family lived in a one-story white house in a poor neighborhood in Washington, D.C.[1]

Hasker Bing was a bricklayer. Dave once said that it was "tough" for his Dad to find work in the winters. "But he always provided enough for us."[2] A few years after Dave was born, another sister, Brenda, and a brother, Hasker, Jr., were born. Yes, the Bings were poor — they had four kids to raise. But, Hasker Bing had a fine heart and a solid head. He told his son that a person's race wasn't important. The person was. He said that nothing in life comes easy. You've got to work hard to get ahead, each and every day.[3]

Spending Time With Family

Hasker Bing practiced what he preached. He was friendly and polite to everyone. No one who knew Hasker Bing ever had a bad word to say about him. Hasker Bing had many talents too. He was a great cook. He was known for his tasty pies. He could also build many things with his hands — from a barbecue pit to a complete house. He worked hard during the week. Then on Sundays, Hasker Bing sang in the church choir. His strong powerful voice could be heard over all the others in the church.[4]

Dave looked up to his father. On weekends the two of them often went fishing. They would take a boat up the Potomac River. They would drop their lines over the side and wait. Hours later they would come home with fish for supper.[5]

Church was very important in the Bing family. The whole family went to the New Mount Olive Baptist Church. They spent a good part of their

Sundays there. Dave went to Sunday School. Like his father, he also joined the choir when he got older. Church values and morals were a given in the Bing family.[6]

Juanita Bing was a strong woman, always positive and loving.[7] She taught Dave and her other children important lessons about life. She used to tell them, "Have respect for others. And if you see anybody that you can help, you try to help them."[8]

Other family members lived nearby. They included Bing cousins, aunts, and uncles. Dave really liked his Uncle John, his father's brother. The family often went on picnics. The kids would run around and play. The adults talked and ate, or relaxed in the shade. Everybody had a good time.[9]

Years later Dave would give his family a lot of credit for helping him to succeed. "I had a mother and father, and they had old-fashioned values. I had caring neighbors and an extended family."[10]

The Most Popular Kid in the Neighborhood

The neighborhood kids all wanted to be around Dave. He was outgoing and had lots of friends.

Dave Bings's mother taught Bing and his brothers and sisters important lessons about life. She stressed the importance of helping others whenever you can. Dave Bing has taken this message into his adult life. The March of Dimes is one of the many organizations he has devoted his time to.

There were always children playing at the Bing house.[11]

Young Dave dreamed of becoming a professional baseball player. He had the grace and speed of a natural athlete. As a kid he played baseball on a Little League team. One day during the playoffs his father came to watch him. This changed their relationship; it made things better between them.

Dave said, "It was the first time our team ever played in a real ballpark. We had a dugout, a real infield, and a fence around the outfield. I hit three home runs out of the park that day." And his father "was swelled with pride, and that made me proud." Dave added, "from that point on, my participation in athletics was something we shared."[12]

Dave grew up playing basketball like thousands of other city kids. The Watts Recreation Center was just around the corner from his house. It had courts and offered basketball lessons. At Watts, Dave learned the basics of the game. Then, at about age twelve, Dave began playing basketball at Kelly Miller Recreation Center. This was at Dave's junior high school. The center was known locally for its basketball team. It was here that Dave improved his playing and learned how to compete.[13]

Dave wasn't really made for basketball. He was shorter than a lot of the other boys his age. But he wanted to be good at this game. He worked harder than some boys twice his height.[14] He listened carefully and practiced the basketball drills over and over. He worked at basketball on the playground and in the gym. As time went on something in Dave made him think that maybe basketball could be the game for him.

High School Basketball

Dave entered Spingarn High School in northeast Washington, D.C., in 1959.[15] Spingarn was just the place for an up-and-coming ball player such as Dave Bing. The school was known for its winning basketball team, called the Green Wave. Every year the Green Wave competed against other city high schools. Almost every year it won the championship. The team coach, William Rountree, drilled his players hard. He wanted the boys to do well—both on and off the court.[16]

The first thing Coach Rountree noticed about Dave Bing was how much he wanted to win. "He was always the first one in my gym class, the first one out on the basketball court—always the first—and the last one to leave."[17]

Coach Rountree also noticed other traits about Dave. He was someone who listened, followed instructions, respected his teachers, and was a good leader. Dave wanted everyone to succeed, not just himself. He was someone willing to bring others along, not shine alone.[18] In high school Dave proved he could be a leader. He became class treasurer, captain of the basketball team, and president of the school's YMCA club (called the Hi-Y Club).[19]

"I've never had anybody like him in all the years I taught," says Coach Rountree. "He did so many things right." Soon Dave's basketball talents started to show. "As we developed systems of play on the basketball court, I could see that Dave had excellent talent in this field," Coach Rountree said. "Every afternoon we'd lock the gym doors and practice. We'd stick at it from about 3:15 P.M. to 4:30 P.M. I'd encourage the boys to give everybody a chance."[20]

Coach Rountree also talked about life. He kept telling the boys that they had to go to class. He also told them that they should go to church and lead a spiritual life. He told them that they should make something of themselves. If one of his players began to cut school, Coach Rountree would show up on the boy's doorstep. He had to find out what was going on.

Most important of all, Coach Rountree told his players to go to college. He told them that if they worked hard and stayed out of trouble, he'd help them go to college. He'd let the colleges know about the good basketball players he had. He'd help his players get scholarships (awards of money) to pay for school.[21] This was a dream for a poor city child such as Dave Bing. Nobody in Dave's family had ever gone to college.[22]

On Friday afternoons at Spingarn, the gym would be packed. The Green Wave would run out, ready to play. The crowd would go wild. The cheerleaders and fans were excited to watch the Green Wave play. Most times Dave's father would be there to watch. The coach always led the team in prayer before the start of a game.[23] The Green Wave did very well when Dave played for them. During one game the team scored more than 100 points. This was the first time the Green Wave had ever done this. They beat Douglass High 108-38. [24]

In his senior year Dave was the Green Wave's highest scorer. He also had the most assists.[25] Dave had athletic ability, style, and the moves that would make him an all-American before he graduated. He could have broken every record in existence. But Coach Rountree didn't want him to be that kind of player. The coach explained,

"I wanted the team to all share the responsibility and the points."[26]

One of Dave's teammates on the Green Wave, Don Hicks, became his best friend. Don describes Dave, whom his friends called "Duke," as the most popular person at Spingarn.[27] Duke had several girlfriends in high school. All of them were very beautiful. In his senior year Dave started dating a pretty, quiet girl named Aaris Young. She was a sophomore. Before long Aaris and Dave introduced Don Hicks to Aaris's best friend, Patricia Green. The four of them spent a lot of time together. They'd go to the local restaurant and order a "teen twist" sandwich and an orange freeze. Or they'd all get in Dave's father's black Ford and go over to the local hangout for teenagers. Sometimes they'd arrive at parties late, "just to be noticed," Don said.

In the summers Dave and Don worked long

hours as bricklayers with Hasker Bing. In their spare time, they'd shoot hoops.[28]

All along Dave Bing knew what he wanted. He wanted to play basketball and go to college. As it turned out, lots of colleges wanted him too. Coaches at many of the schools had heard about the Spingarn team. They had also heard about Dave Bing.

Coach Rountree says, "College coaches came to me from all over trying to get Dave. By the time he left, he was real experienced. And they wanted him because he had the combination—academically and in leadership and basketball."[29] By now Bing was an honor student with a 3.1 grade average.[30]

Bing admits that he was offered "better than 100 college scholarships."[31] He had his heart set on Princeton. But Princeton didn't accept him.

"For the first time in my life I was rejected because somebody told me that I wasn't good enough," Bing said years later. "I was devastated! I decided to enter my second choice, Syracuse University, and I made up my mind that I would never again put myself in a position where I would have to face rejection."[32]

Dave Bing faced rejection for the first time in his life when Princeton University didn't accept him. Syracuse University, his second choice, was where Bing ended up going to college and playing college basketball.

COLLEGE DAYS

Central New York State was very different from the inner city streets of Washington, D.C., where Dave Bing had grown up. There were farms and lakes everywhere. There was also the city of Syracuse, home of Syracuse University.

The school has stood on the same hill since it opened in 1870. The campus is pretty with gray stone buildings around a grassy, tree-shaded square. The students' housing is just past the square.[1] When Dave Bing arrived in the fall of 1962, workers were finishing the new Manley Field House. It had a brand new basketball court.

Bing would soon be spending many hours at Manley.[2]

A Whole New World

Syracuse was a whole new world for Dave Bing. He had grown up in a neighborhood where everyone was the same color as he. He had always gone to schools with mostly black students. But at Syracuse most students were white. In 1962 only about one hundred of the eleven thousand students on campus were black.[3] Like Dave Bing, most of the black men there were athletes. Some people were afraid that the black students would not do well at Syracuse. These people were afraid that inner city schools hadn't prepared the black students well enough for college.[4]

Dave Bing remembers his reaction to this new world. "I accepted it as a challenge and applied the same competitive attitude I had on the basketball court to the classroom. I wanted to prove that I could compete with people from all over the country—I refused to accept that they were better or smarter than I."[5]

Friends and Fun

Dave Bing picked up tips on how to study from his roommate, Frank Nicoletti. Frank was a very good student. He came from Weehawken, New Jersey. He had been voted an All-American basketball player at his Catholic prep school. Despite their outer differences, the two young men got along well. Dave Bing copied Frank's way of studying. In return, he enjoyed giving Frank advice about girls and dating. This was something that the priests at his Catholic high school hadn't taught Frank much about.[6]

The two young men were always playing jokes on each other. As Frank tells it, "Dave had a reputation for washing his face, saying his prayers, and being a gentleman. I got a reputation as a troublemaker."

Frank goes on to reveal the "true" Dave Bing. "But Dave's a sneaky guy. I'd be walking down the dorm hall to the bathroom and Dave would roll five [noisy] cans down the hall. I'd see what was happening, so I'd race back to the room in order to avoid getting caught. But the resident adviser would come out, see me, and put me on probation. And just as the adviser entered the room, Dave would be kneeling down praying."

The jokes went on. But Frank had his ways of getting even. "Dave got involved with the ROTC on campus for a while," Frank says. (ROTC stands for Reserve Officers Training Corps. It trains students in schools, colleges, and universities to become officers in the United States armed services. It tries to develop students for positions of military leadership during national emergencies.) The ROTC practiced drills first thing in the morning. Frank said, "I used to change Dave's alarm clock so it would go off at 5:00 A.M. instead of 7:00 A.M. He'd get up and rush outside to the quadrangle and then he'd be the only one out there. It was often 10 degrees below zero."[7]

The two men are still friends today. Dave Bing's father had been right. Race didn't matter — people did.

Bing might have been a joker. But, he was very serious about getting good grades. He went to all his classes. He hardly missed a single one in four years. He studied late into the night. In his spare time, he'd listen to music.

Dave Bing quietly earned the respect of those around him. "One of the great things about Dave was the level of maturity he had," commented his former basketball teammate, Jim Boeheim. "He was looked up to so much because of the great way he dealt with people. He captained the basketball team three years in a row, which was very unusual. And he became the leader on campus."[8]

Before Dave Bing got there, Syracuse had the worst basketball record of any college in the country. It was strictly a football school.[9] But that was going to change. The university had hired a new coach, Fred Lewis. They told him to put together a winning basketball team. Fred Lewis went on to do just that. In the spring of 1962, Lewis went to Washington, D.C. to recruit Dave Bing. Bing, who had his heart set on Princeton, hadn't even thought about Syracuse as a possibility. But the coach talked him into it. He told Dave Bing he would be a key player if he came to the school.[10]

Just as with his studies, Bing worked hard at basketball. Freshmen (first-year students) had their own team. Training was tiring. The team practiced every afternoon from mid-October to late March. They worked for more than three hours a day. They ran laps around the track or ran sprints. They also exercised with weights and rebound machines. They even worked with basketballs that didn't bounce. Over and over, the team would practice and go through plays. Often the freshmen team would take on the varsity in practice games. As Jim Boeheim puts it, "We beat them every time."[11]

A Winning Season

By the end of his first season at Syracuse, Dave Bing had proven himself. He had led the team "in every offensive department." "He finished with a 25.7 scoring average."[12]

Dave Bing was an unforgettable sight on the basketball court. He stood 6 feet, 3 inches tall and weighed about 180 pounds.[13] His hair was cut short in the popular style of the day.[14] His body was well toned and well muscled, and his facial features were well defined.[15]

Frank Nicoletti recalls how Dave Bing "just exploded" on the court at game time. He had skills that "no one came close to matching." He was a good athlete. He also knew how to be a winner. He jumped high in the air to rebound the ball. He could hang in the air and just slam-dunk the ball in the basket without even looking. The crowd that packed into Manley Field House would go wild.[16]

Syracuse athletes were known as the Orange Men. When the "Orange" team wasn't playing at Manley, they went to other schools. They went to Philadelphia, West Virginia, and even as far as southern California for a National College Athletic Association (NCAA) tournament. Practices or tournaments were even held during Thanksgiving and Christmas vacations. There were very few breaks from the routine.[17]

Dave Bing broke just about every school basketball record at Syracuse. He scored the most points in a college career—1,883.[18] During his senior year he averaged close to 30 points a game.[19] He became one of the best college basketball players in the country. He was voted an All-American during his junior and senior years.[20]

Still, Bing kept his vow to study hard. He knew playing basketball wasn't going to be his life forever. But a good education would last for life. He was doing solid work and making decent grades. These things would be important after basketball.

Dave Bing's athletic ability on the court at Syracuse was unforgettable. Even after he left the University, Bing (second from left, row 2) still attended charity functions to benefit children.

Starting a Family

During college another big change happened in Bing's life. He had quietly married his high school sweetheart, Aaris. She had given birth to two young daughters—Cassandra, 2, and Bridgett, 6 months. By his senior year they were living in a small apartment in Syracuse.[21]

In the spring of 1966, Dave Bing played his final college basketball game. Syracuse was playing Colgate, and Manley Field House was filled with 7,105 fans. Before the game started, an announcement was made. A student presented Dave Bing with a plaque of thanks from the entire student body. Smiling proudly, Bing stood on the court. A loud roar of applause rose from the bleachers. His teammates, friends, and fans clapped and cheered. The Orange Men went on to defeat Colgate, 122-88.[22]

MOVING ON
TO THE PROS

One of the many people watching Dave
Bing play basketball during his senior
year at Syracuse was Earl Lloyd. Back in
1950 Lloyd had been one of the first African
Americans to play professional basketball.
He had since gone on to run a car company
in Detroit. But he still helped find
up-and-coming young players for the Detroit
Pistons. Earl Lloyd's job was to discover
college players who had the talent for
professional basketball. He watched Dave
Bing twirl, dive, jump, and slam-dunk the
ball. He knew he'd found a great player.[1]

Playing for the Pistons

At the time the rules for signing up new players were fairly strict. The NBA team that finished the season in last place got first draft pick. In 1966 the Pistons had finished close to last. They had had one of the worst seasons in NBA history.[2] The team's first choice for a new player was Cazzie Russell. He was an All-American player from the University of Michigan, and he was a local hero in Detroit. Dave Bing was the Pistons' second choice. However, as luck would have it, the New York Knicks got first pick. They chose Cazzie Russell. Dave Bing went to Detroit.[3]

Earl Lloyd was one of the few people in Detroit not sorry about losing Cazzie Russell to New York. He says, "I knew we were getting a very very special person, an outstanding basketball player, with twice the character."[4]

So in the summer of 1966 Dave Bing, Aaris, and their children moved to the Detroit suburbs. They found a small, three-bedroom house on a quiet, tree-shaded street.[5]

Training camp began in September. Then in October, Bing started his first regular season. He would play the guard position with the Pistons. At first things didn't go well. In the opening game against the Cincinnati Royals, he accidentally knocked down the team's star player, Oscar Robertson. Robertson wouldn't let Bing get away with that mistake. He helped make sure that Bing didn't score a single point.[6]

Dave Bing was trying too hard to prove himself. He knew that the Pistons had really wanted Cazzie Russell. "I knew what the Detroit fans thought of Cazzie. And I thought of it constantly," he later told a reporter.[7] He confessed to some of his old college friends, "I've been too anxious...I haven't played as well as I know I can."[8]

Soon after the Cincinnati game, the Pistons would play the Los Angeles Lakers in Detroit. Dave Bing would show the fans why they didn't need to dream about Cazzie Russell anymore. Bing took off as soon as the game began. He was everywhere the ball was. Mel Allen, a Syracuse student at that game, said, "His shots poured in—from the corners, from the key—he drove for layups. Eight times he stole rebounds...."[9]

When the game was over the Pistons had won. Dave Bing had won, too. He was no longer a player with doubts. He had played one of his best games yet. He had scored 35 points.

Dave Bing may not have been the Detroit fans' first choice,
but he won them over with his talent.

By the end of that first season Bing had averaged 20 points per game. He won the title of NBA Rookie of the Year.[10] The following year he led the NBA in scoring. In fifty games he scored 1,371 points, averaging 27.4 points a game.[11]

"That is no small achievement, because usually guards don't lead the league in scoring," said Earl Lloyd.[12]

Dave Bing became the Pistons Most Valuable Player (MVP) in January 1968.[13] The Pistons began winning for the first time in over ten years. Once only five thousand people had come to the team's games. Now the Pistons had Dave Bing and a new winning streak. More than ten thousand people now attended the Pistons' games.[14]

Dave Bing was an All-Star player for seven straight seasons. One of his best games was the NBA's All-Star game in January 1968. He grabbed the ball from the other team and jumped in for a lay-up. But his shot was blocked. Still in mid-leap, he quickly wrenched himself around. He switched the ball from his left to right hand, and dropped a clean shot from a new angle.[15]

People couldn't help but notice Dave Bing's incredible speed. As Earl Lloyd once said, "He

Dave Bing became the Pistons' Most Valuable player in January, 1968. He went on, however, to become a Pistons legend.

knew only one speed—fast." Added to that was his quick timing on the court. "He was poetry in motion," Lloyd recalled.[16]

Ken Hudson, a referee, also remembers how Dave moved the ball down the court. He was like a freewheeling whirlwind the one time Hudson watched him. "He must have done twelve twists and flips," Hudson later said. "I was in awe. It was an incredible move."[17]

Time magazine reported how Bing "slides past, spins around, or ducks under bigger, clumsier defenders." The article continued, "He also has fantastic spring. When he uncoils and jumps, his hands reach twelve feet into the air."[18]

Follow the Leader

Dave Bing's honesty and ability to lead under pressure were remarkable as well. Instead of fighting dirty or being out just for himself, Earl Lloyd said, "when things got rough, he would take his game to another level. He would not buckle under pressure, but would help others to play better and bring them along with him."[19]

In those days a professional basketball player had no choice about what team he played on. He was traded or bought by a team whether he wanted to play for them or not. Dave Bing stayed with the Pistons for nine years. In 1975 he was sent to the Washington Bullets. He stayed with this team until 1977. Then he moved to the Boston Celtics for a year.[20]

Dave Bing traveled for months during the season. From late October until late spring, he'd be on the road. Restaurants, hotels, gyms—that's where NBA players spent most of their time. They hardly ever had a day off. Their schedule was hectic. A player had to be ready for each game. Even if he didn't feel like playing ball, he still had to tie his sneakers and go out on the court.[21]

The teams Dave Bing played on never won any championships. Maybe this was good. It taught him how to deal with the ups and downs of winning and losing. "You're on a high one night and in the pits the next," he says. Basketball is the kind of game where "you can have individual success, and [still] your team loses."[22]

He wasn't making a lot of money either. Today NBA top players earn millions of dollars. But that wasn't true when Dave Bing began playing. His starting salary was $15,000.[23] "I wasn't making enough money to support my family," he said later. "I realized then that an athlete's playing life is short-lived and fragile."[24]

Some companies asked Dave Bing if he would advertise their products on television. Many well-known players do this. But Bing turned down the offers. He didn't want to allow himself to be used.[25]

Instead, Dave Bing was getting ready to leave professional sports. He still traveled around the country playing basketball. But, he also became an incredible reader. He himself guesses that he read somewhere between 200 and 300 books in a season.[26] They covered all sorts of subjects. He also took jobs during off-seasons. He needed the money to support his family. But he was also learning. He worked first at the National Bank of Detroit. For seven summers he worked in the bank's training program.[27] Each year he tried a different job. He started off as a teller. He ended up as a manager. Banking taught him a lot about how business works. "Everything revolves around finance in business," Bing noted. Banking taught him how the real world works.[28]

"I think many athletes make the common

Dave Bing always knew that his basketball career would not last forever. He needed to decide what he would do after basketball. When he speaks to groups of young people today, he stresses the fact that an education is important. He also reminds the listeners that it's o.k. to dream about being a professional athlete. But, you also need to have skills you can use in every day life.

mistake of associating only with a small group of people," says Bing; namely, "people like them who are involved in sports. This causes them to stop growing as a person." He says that working at a "normal" job during the off-season didn't let him do this. "I had to get up every morning and be at work at a specific time like everyone else. I also had an hour for lunch, and there was no bending the rules."[29]

Life After Basketball

Dave Bing kept learning. "I knew my days in the NBA were soon to end, and I needed to decide what I would do for a second career," he said.[30] For two more years he worked in a program run by Chrysler Corporation, training car dealers.

After all this, Dave Bing knew he didn't want to be a banker. "Bankers sit behind a desk all day; I'm a people person," he said.[31] And "I didn't want to be a car dealer either. So I began thinking about what would be available when I retired, and I started to look around." [32]

Bing's time with the Celtics, 1977–1978, was his last season with the NBA. Dave Bing was

During his twelve years in basketball, Dave Bing (standing, second from right) scored just over twenty points a game each season on average. He went on to play on a team of fellow legends of the NBA.

ready to spend more time with his family and to try something else.[33]

He had been injured playing basketball. He'd had twenty-eight stitches in his face. And his fingers on his right hand had been jammed so much that he used to wear a sponge taped to his knuckles for protection.[34] The worst injury may have been during the 1971–1972 season, when someone accidentally poked a finger in his eye. He was in the hospital for that injury, and he missed some game time.[35]

During his twelve years in basketball, Dave Bing scored just over 20 points a game per season on average.[36] His total number of points scored was more than 18,000. That made him one of the NBA's top scorers. In 1976 he was voted the NBA All-Star Game Most Valuable Player.[37] Now it was time to move on. Whatever came next, Dave Bing was ready.

LIFE AFTER THE NBA

The time had come to choose a career. Dave Bing got a job with a steel company in Detroit called Paragon Steel. He went through the company's training program and worked in many different departments.[1] He needed to figure out what kind of work suited him best.

After a few years of learning he wanted more. He had a lot of energy, and he was unhappy without a challenge. Working for someone else might be fine for other people. But not for Dave Bing. There had to be something more—something he could do on his own.[2]

Starting a Business

Finally, by 1980, he had decided what he would do. He'd run his own steel company in Detroit. Of course, starting your own company takes money. You need to rent office space. You also need to pay for equipment, and advertise. Bing had saved some money from his NBA days, but he needed more. At first bankers weren't sure about loaning money to Bing. "People thought I was already rich," he says.[3] Eventually he was able to borrow what he needed.

Bing Steel started with just four workers in a small rented office. Bing also rented a warehouse. He would find companies, usually car makers, that needed steel. Then he would find the steel makers and work with them to fill the orders he had. Soon he bought his own plant and began working with the steel instead of buying it. He cut, shaped, and bent rolls of the metal himself.[4]

As Dave Bing found out, breaking into the business world on your own is hard. He had many problems. "My first year, I lost $100,000. I expected to lose money, but I didn't expect to lose that much."[5]

Dave Bing remembers how scared he was. "It was a very frightening experience to lose 60

Dave Bing (second from left) was inducted into the Afro American Sports Hall of Fame, following his record-making career. Even as a Hall of Famer, he had a hard time getting people to lend him money for his new business.

percent of my equity [money] in such a short period. This was hard-earned money that took me twelve years to accumulate [build up] during my professional basketball career." He adds, "Not only did I lose money, but during the first year I didn't draw a salary from the business. So I suffered a loss of income to boot."[6]

Another challenge Bing had to overcome was the way many people looked at him. According to Bing, "When most people look at former athletes, they don't take them seriously. They take them to be dumb, spoiled, and lazy."[7]

To make matters worse, he was new to the steel business. He was not known in the field. He was also an African American—doing something that few African Americans did. He talks about how it was. "There were many times I was kept waiting for hours in a lobby. Whether they were sending me a message, I don't know. But I had the patience to wait them out."[8]

By the second year, things started to get better. Dave Bing gives his quality product the credit. That year, Bing Steel would do business with General Motors. This helped his company. By the late 1980s sales were up to $45 million.[9]

Dave Bing (second from left) is shown here standing next to Muhammed Ali, as Dave Bing Day was proclaimed a holiday in Detroit on February 11, 1991.

Today there are fifty workers at Bing Steel. They work out of two warehouses and in an office.[10]

In 1985 Dave Bing started another company called Superb Manufacturing. It makes special steel parts for cars. The parts are sold to major car makers such as Ford and Chrysler. About 150 people work there. The company makes about $35 million.[11]

Dave Bing gives his work today the same kind of energy he once gave to basketball. He's at work by 7:30 A.M. every day and often stays until 7:00 P.M.[12] "Sixty– to seventy–hour work weeks are pretty normal for me," he says.[13] When he gets home at night, he reads the paper, maybe watches a bit of television, and then he's in bed by 9:00 P.M.[14]

Bing says, "I take the responsibility very seriously. I try to lead by example more than anything else."[15] Bing has a warm way with people. He knows all his workers. When he walks through one of his factories he calls them by name. He shakes their hands and asks about their families. He also pays them above average. He promotes those employees who work hard.[16] Apparently his parent's lessons about treating people with respect have carried over into Bing's business life.

Helping the Workers

About 80 percent of Bing's workers are African Americans. He helps everyone work together as a team. He wants them to do well. "I want to build my business so it can provide jobs for blacks," Bing says. "In my organization I let them know that, with proper education, preparation, and effort, they can...become an important part of this company."[17]

One worker who has done that is Rai Withers. She started out as a secretary in 1980. She was one of the four original Bing Steel workers. Today she has an important job. She is in charge of buying all of the steel for the company, a total of 10,000 tons a month.

Withers says, "I came up through the ranks. We've had guys who worked in the plant, and we saw that they had potential. We trained them and sent them to school. And since then we've promoted them, as well." She adds that she is unique only in that she started with the company

About 80 percent of Dave Bing's workers are African Americans. He lets his workers know that with hard work and dedication they can grow with his company.

at the very beginning. "The opportunity to succeed is presented to all employees here."

Rai Withers has great respect for Dave Bing. "He has an aura about him. When he enters a room, you know you're looking at a person who's important, who has it under control."[18]

Dave Bing does have "it under control." When Bing Steel was going through hard times, he thought of giving up. The bad times didn't seem to end. But he stuck it out and things started to turn around. Bing credits the discipline he acquired as an athlete for helping him through such rough times.[19]

Withers says, "He's got a keen awareness of the business of being in business. I've seen him grow immensely as a professional. He's always reading something. He's always on top of current events."[20]

In recent years he has done very well. His companies are often listed among the most successful black-owned businesses in the country.[21] In 1984 Dave Bing was invited to the White House where President Reagan presented him with two awards.[22]

Still, even with all his successes, Dave Bing can be as easy-going as the next guy. At company

In 1984, Dave Bing (shaking hands with President Reagan) was invited to the White House where the president presented him with the National Minority Small Business Person of the Year Award.

get-togethers, such as the annual picnic, Bing will wander over to get something to drink. Then he'll settle down in the shade of a tree. Often he'll become so relaxed that he will fall asleep.[23]

The years have not changed Dave Bing all that much. He is still thin, and he moves with ease.[24] His long-time friend, Don Hicks sometimes comes to visit him in Detroit. The two often play tennis together. Don Hicks says of Dave Bing, "He's still in great shape and can move quite fast." [25]

Dave Bing has worked long and hard to get where he is today. He gives a great deal of time and energy to his work. But he keeps a clear head about it all. "I haven't gotten hung up on the business success," he says.[26] "I want to succeed so I can be a good role model and have a positive impact on my community."[27]

WORKING
WITH PEOPLE

D ave Bing's mother used to tell young Dave, "If you see anybody that you can help, you try to help them."[1]

Dave Bing himself said, "The way I was taught and raised is that you can never forget where you came from. You've always got to go back and help."[2] Bing began doing this when he played for the Pistons. In 1968 he was invited to speak at a dinner given by Big Brothers. He accepted the invitation. He was impressed by what Big Brothers was doing. The group was finding men who would be willing to serve in a "big brother" role to young boys who needed support.

Helping Others

Bing said, "I became a big brother. In five years I had three little brothers." He did all sorts of things with the boys. He notes, "We all became friends. I took them on field trips and to sporting events. I visited them in their homes. We went out to eat at restaurants." As proof of Dave Bing's lasting impact on these three boys, he notes, "They're all grown and have families of their own now. I'm very close to them."[3] Bing also helped his three "brothers" to become involved with basketball. One way he did this was to take them for a week to the mountains of Pennsylvania.

Basketball Camp

Bing and a partner, Howie Landa, a college basketball coach, started the Dave Bing All-Pro Basketball Camp in Pennsylvania. The camp sits on over one hundred acres of land. When they bought the land in 1968, it already had a dining hall, cabins, and a pool. They added basketball courts. Then they found inner city kids, both girls and boys, aged eight to sixteen or so. The kids came from Detroit, New York City, Washington,

D.C., and New Jersey. Dave Bing offered to help pay the way for those kids who couldn't afford the fee for the camp. The camp didn't make any money for him. But it was a place for the young people to improve their basketball skills. Bing himself was at the camp for four to six weeks every summer. He hired college basketball players as counselors. He also got some of the big names in basketball to show how they played and to talk with the campers.

Learning More Than Ball Playing

The campers learned more than just the right moves on the court. They learned about teamwork; they learned about working together. They would grow not only as athletes, but as human beings too.

"I had ten campers who later went on to play professional basketball in the NBA," Bing notes with pride. Dave Bing stuck with his camp even after he retired from basketball. But in 1980, when he started up Bing Steel, he had to leave. His new business took up all of his time.

Today he still has good memories about the camp. "I've had great relationships with a lot of the kids who came. I had something to do with their development, and I'm still in touch with many of them today."[4]

Giving up his camp didn't mean Dave Bing would not be involved with young people. Just a few years ago he made many of the 4,500 students in the Detroit Public Schools very happy. The city suddenly had run out of money. It couldn't afford to pay for the costs of the many sports programs in the schools.[5] To a lot of inner city kids, sports was the only reason they went to school. Dave Bing heard about the problem. He was concerned. He feared that many kids would drop out of school if there were no sports programs. He decided to do something about it.

Saving Detroit's School Sports Programs

Dave Bing collected money from local businesses, charities, and sports teams. The Pistons put on a game against an NBA All-Star team led by Magic Johnson. The team gave the money it made to Bing's cause. They raised close to $300,000.[6] Altogether, Dave Bing raised about $600,000. This was enough to save the school sports

When Dave Bing talks to young people, he is careful to point out that the dream of playing professional sports is not going to come true for very many people. It is important to plan for the future.

programs.[7] He saved school sports because, as he said, "Without them I don't think some kids would be motivated to attend school."[8]

Speaking Out at Schools

Bing Still works with the local public schools. He says, "I enjoy speaking at graduations. I go to career days and to Black History Month."[9] Why does he do this? He explains:

"Kids need to see that there are community people concerned about them and willing to give them their time."[10]

"These kids are too young to remember me and my [basketball] playing days, but I can give them the picture of what it was like. They look at me at first when I come in and ask themselves, 'Who is this old guy?' They ask how many points I made and [other] questions about my basketball playing. Once I've answered those, they are thinking, 'This guy had a pretty good career,' and they're a little more receptive [eager to listen]."[11]

Bing tells young people all about his basketball days. But he points out that the dream of playing professional sports is not going to come

Dave Bing devotes a great deal of his time to young people. He works with the Boy Scouts, the Boys and Girls Club of southeastern Michigan, and with Junior Achievement. His main goal is to be a role model.

true for very many of them. Even if they do get there, he tells the young people, they have a whole life ahead of them beyond that. It is still important to study and plan for the future. "If you put forth the same effort to become a good student, you can succeed in other fields he often tells the students."[12]

Dave Bing is still very involved with young people. He works with the Boy Scouts, and the Boys and Girls Club of Southeastern Michigan, as well as Junior Achievement. He believes these groups offer programs "that can play a role in helping kids develop."[13]

Dave Bing sees many young people who remind him of himself. They are growing up poor in the inner city. They go to public schools. He tells them that they can succeed. He tells them to work hard. "I don't accept excuses from them," he says.[14]

Dave Bing helps out in other ways too. He gives his time to more than a dozen other local groups. Some of these include the Detroit Black United Fund and the Michigan Minority Business Development Council.

Dave Bing has said that his main goal is to be a good role model. It would seem that he has achieved his goal. In 1985 Detroit gave him the city's Humanitarian of the Year Award. This award is a way of saying "thank you" for all that he has given and continues to give to the people in his community.[15]

THINKING AHEAD

Today, Dave Bing's life is a full one. He is at his office sixty or more hours a week. Then he spends another fifteen hours a week with his volunteer work. Bing takes one day a week, Sunday, for himself. He goes to the Hartford Memorial Baptist Church in midtown Detroit. He loves to "get energized with the singing, the sermon, the fellowship."[1]

Over the years life has not always been easy for Dave Bing. He and Aaris were divorced, and a second marriage has also ended in divorce. But Bing remains on friendly terms with his ex-wives.

Dave Bing is a very busy man. He spends sixty or more hours a week at his office and another fifteen hours a week doing his volunteer work. He is shown here raisng money at a 1990 Easter Seals telethon.

He is also close to the three daughters he and Aaris had together.[2]

A Family Man

Bing is very proud of his daughters. "I have three daughters I've never had any problems with. All went to college and never gave me any trouble. All are working with me in the business," he says.[3]

His middle daughter, Bridgett says of her dad, "He was always even-tempered, even with three girls."[4]

Dave Bing says, "A high point in my life now is my first grandchild" (Bridgett's little boy, Kenneth David, who is five).[5]

Dave Bing clearly gives to more than just his family. He also gives to friends. He has a heart "about the size of a lion," says Earl Lloyd.[6] For instance not too long ago, Dave Bing's friend Don Hicks had more bills than he could pay. He couldn't afford to buy a house. He and his wife had been living with his mother for many years. Dave Bing told him to write down everything he owed, to the penny, and send the list to him. Don Hicks did and says, "I guess in about two or three days, the check was in my mailbox." Dave Bing had paid off all of Don's bills for him.[7]

Once about six years ago, the man who kept all of the team records for the Pistons, Morris Moorawnick, had a stroke. He and Dave Bing had known each other for a long time. They were friendly, but not very close. Dave Bing showed up at the hospital to visit Moorawnick, who said, "He's that kind of person. I would expect that of Dave Bing."[8]

One of the best moments in Dave Bing's life was being named to the Basketball Hall of Fame in May 1990. This is one of the highest honors in any sport. The ceremony took place at the Hall of Fame in Springfield, Massachusetts. Don Hicks and Coach Rountree came all the way from Washington, D.C.[9]

Many other honors and awards have come to Dave Bing. His office and home are overflowing with plaques and trophies of all kinds.[10] Most recently he was given the George Arents Pioneer Medal. This is Syracuse University's top award for former students who are well-known for what they do.[11]

These are exciting times for Dave Bing. He has big plans for Superb Manufacturing. He is

Dave Bing (first, from left to right) was named to the Basketball Hall of Fame in May of 1990. This is one of the highest honors for players in any sport.

going to combine it with a Detroit plastics company. This will put the company in a good position in the car parts industry. This will also mean building two more factories and buying more land on the east side of Detroit. Bing is excited about the future.[12]

Dave Bing wants to be right up there with the winners, just as he was once on the basketball court. Today the "game" is a bit harder for him. But the demands are similar. He still needs speed and quick wits. These are things that Dave Bing has.[13]

As Rai Withers says of Dave Bing, "You better keep your eye on him, because you don't know what he's going to do next."[14]

CHRONOLOGY

1943—Dave Bing born on November 29 in Washington, D.C.

1962–1966—Bing attends Syracuse University.

1966–1978—Bing plays NBA basketball for Detroit Pistons, Washington Bullets, Boston Celtics.

1980—Bing founds Bing Steel in Detroit, Michigan.

1985—Bing founds Superb Manufacturing in Detroit.

1989—Bing raises money to save the sports program in the Detroit Public Schools.

1990—Bing inducted into Basketball Hall of Fame.

1995—Bing on board of directors of "Midnight Basketball" program. Organized to keep teens off the streets and away from trouble.

CHAPTER NOTES

Chapter 1

1. Mel R. Allen, "Going to See Dave," *Syracuse Magazine*, Spring 1994, p. 22. Date and game score from personal interview with Morris Moorawnick, Pistons' statistician, May 13, 1994.

2. "The Pistons' Bing," *Newsweek*, January 8, 1968, p. 68.

3. Robert L. Shook and Ramon Greenwood, *The Name of the Game Is Life* (Chicago: Contemporary Books, 1992), p. 15.

4. Ibid.; Personal interview with Earl Lloyd, April 7, 1994.

5. Dave Bing resume.

6. Rick Telander, "Life Lessons from a Man of Steel," *Sports Illustrated*, August 19, 1991, p. 48.

7. Editors of Time-Life Books, *African-Americans: Voices of Triumph, Leadership* (Alexandria, Va.: Time-Life Books, 1994), p. 111. Statistics from *Black Enterprise* (June 1993), p. 81.

8. Personal interview with Frank Nicoletti, April 27, 1994, and with Dave Bing, May 2, 1994.

9. Shook and Greenwood, p. 33.

Chapter 2

1. Personal interview with Juanita Bing, April 7, 1994, and Dave Bing resume.

2. Bob Snyder, "Bing Takes Fame in Stride," *Syracuse Herald-American, Empire Magazine,* February 20, 1966, p. 11.

3. Mel R. Allen, "Going to See Dave," *Syracuse Magazine,* Spring 1994, p. 20.

4. Personal interview with Don Hicks, April 13, 1994.

5. Personal interview with Juanita Bing, April 7, 1994, and with William Rountree, April 8, 1994.

6. Personal interview with Juanita Bing, April 7, 1994, and with Don Hicks, April 13, 1994.

7. Personal interview with Don Hicks, April 13, 1994.

8. Personal interview with Juanita Bing, April 7, 1994.

9. Ibid.

10. Rick Telander, "Life Lessons From A Man of Steel," *Sports Illustrated,* August 19, 1991, p. 50.

11. Personal interview with Juanita Bing, April 7, 1994.

12. Robert L. Shook and Ramon Greenwood, *The Name of the Game Is Life* (Chicago: Contemporary Books, 1992), pp. 15-16.

13. Personal interview with Don Hicks, April 27, 1994.

14. Personal interview with William Rountree, April 8, 1994.

15. Personal interview with Sue Ray, April 11, 1994.

16. Personal interview with William Rountree, April 8, 1994; "Spingarn Has More Than 100 Points," *The Washington Post*, December 12, 1961.

17. Personal interview with William Rountree, April 8, 1994.

18. Ibid.

19. Personal interview with Sue Ray, April 11, 1994, and with William Rountree, April 8, 1994.

20. Personal interview with William Rountree, April 8, 1994.

21. Ibid.

22. Shook and Greenwood, p. 18.

23. Personal interview with William Rountree, April 8, 1994.

24. "Spingarn Has More Than 100 Points," *The Washington Post*, December 12, 1961.

25. Shook and Greenwood, p. 16.

26. Personal interview with William Rountree, April 8, 1994.

27. Personal interview with Don Hicks, April 27, 1994.

28. Ibid.

29. Personal interview with William Rountree, April 8, 1994.

30. Shook and Greenwood, p. 16.

31. Snyder, p. 11.

32. Shook and Greenwood, p. 17.

Chapter 3

1. *Webster's Collegiate Dictionary*, p. 1513; personal interview with Diane Sloan, Public Relations Office, Syracuse University, April 15, 1994.

2. Personal interview with Frank Nicoletti, April 27, 1994; Rod Macdonald, *Syracuse Basketball, 1900-1975* (Syracuse, N.Y.: Syracuse University, 1975), p. 68.

3. Robert L. Shook and Ramon Greenwood, *The Name of the Game Is Life* (Chicago:

Contemporary Books, 1992), p. 19; personal interview with Diane Sloan, April 15, 1994.

4. Shook and Greenwood, p. 19.

5. Ibid.

6. Ibid.; personal interview with Frank Nicoletti, April 27, 1994.

7. Personal interview with Frank Nicoletti, April 27, 1994.

8. Personal interview with Jim Boeheim, April 27, 1994.

9. Personal interview with Frank Nicoletti, April 27, 1994.

10. Macdonald, pp. 67-68.

11. Ibid.; personal interview with Frank Nicoletti, April 27, 1994.

12. *Onondagan* (Syracuse, N.Y.: Syracuse University, 1963), p. 92.

13. Shook and Greenwood, p. 26.

14. Personal interview with Don Hicks, April 27, 1994.

15. Mel R. Allen, "Going to See Dave," *Syracuse Magazine*, Spring 1994, p. 20.

16. Ibid.; personal interview with Frank Nicoletti, April 27, 1994.

17. Personal interview with Frank Nicoletti,

April 27, 1994; personal interview with Jim Boeheim, April 27, 1994.

18. Allen, p. 20; "Arents Pioneer Medal Winners," *Syracuse Magazine*, Spring 1994, p. 50.

19. Ibid.

20. Shook and Greenwood, p. 20.

21. Bob Snyder, "Bing Takes Fame in Stride," *Syracuse Herald-American, Empire Magazine*, February 20, 1966; Allen, p. 22.

22. *Onondagan*, p. 217.

Chapter 4

1. Personal interview with Earl Lloyd, April 7, 1994.

2. Ibid.; Mel R. Allen, "Going to See Dave," *Syracuse Magazine*, Spring 1994, p. 22.

3. Personal interview with Earl Lloyd, April 7, 1994; "The Pistons' Bing," *Newsweek*, January 8, 1968, p. 68.

4. Personal interview with Earl Lloyd, April 7, 1994.

5. Allen, p. 22.

6. Allen, pp. 20, 22; personal interview with Earl Lloyd, April 7, 1994.

7. *Newsweek*, p. 68.

8. Allen, p. 22.

9. Ibid.

10. Robert L. Shook and Ramon Greenwood, *The Name of the Game Is Life* (Chicago: Contemporary Books, 1992), p. 21; "Power for the Pistons," *Time*, February 2, 1968, p. 45.

11. *Time*, p. 45.

12. Personal interview with Earl Lloyd, April 7, 1994.

13. *Newsweek*, p. 68.

14. *Time*, p. 45.

15. Ibid.

16. Personal interview with Earl Lloyd, April 7, 1994.

17. Ibid.

18. *Time*, p. 45.

19. Personal interview with Earl Lloyd, April 7, 1994.

20. Shook and Greenwood, p. 15.

21. Personal interview with Earl Lloyd, April 7, 1994.

22. Bob Woods, "Still Proving His Mettle," *Sports Illustrated*, Special Advertising Section, November 1992.

23. Shook and Greenwood, p. 21.

24. Morin Bishop, "Ex-Pro Basketball Star

Dave Bing Now Scores His Points in Business," *Sports Illustrated*, April 8, 1985, p. 22.

25. Shook and Greenwood, p. 22

26. Rick Telander, "Life Lessons From a Man of Steel," *Sports Illustrated*, August 19, 1991, p. 49.

27. Tom Henderson, "Dave Bing's Best Turnaround," *Corporate Detroit*, October 1991, p. 38.

28. Shook and Greenwood, p. 22.

29. Ibid., p. 23.

30. Ibid.

31. Henderson, p. 38.

32. Shook and Greenwood, p. 23.

33. Personal interview with Earl Lloyd, April 7, 1994.

34. *Time*, p. 45.

35. Personal interview with Earl Lloyd, April 7, 1994; personal interview with Don Hicks, April 27, 1994.

36. Personal interview with Earl Lloyd, April 7, 1994.

37. Arthur R. Ashe, Jr., *A Hard Road To Glory, Basketball: The African-American Athlete in Basketball* (New York: Amistad, 1993), pp. 75, 86.

Chapter 5

1. Tom Henderson, "Dave Bing's Best Turnaround," *Corporate Detroit Magazine*, October 1991, p. 38.

2. Personal interview with Rai Withers, April 19, 1994; personal interview with Earl Lloyd, April 7, 1994.

3. Rick Telander, "Life Lessons From a Man of Steel," *Sports Illustrated*, August 19, 1991, p. 50.

4. Morin Bishop, "Ex-Pro Basketball Star Dave Bing Now Scores His Points in Business," *Sports Illustrated*, April 8, 1985, p. 22; Robert L. Shook and Ramon Greenwood, *The Name of the Game Is Life* (Chicago: Contemporary Books, 1992), p. 26.

5. Henderson, p. 39.

6. Shook and Greenwood, p. 26.

7. Henderson, p. 38.

8. Ibid., p. 39.

9. Ibid.

10. Personal interview with Rai Withers, April 19, 1994.

11. Henderson, p. 40; personal interview with Dave Bing, May 2, 1994.

12. Henderson, p. 37; personal interview with Don Hicks, April 13, 1994.

13. Personal interview with Dave Bing, May 2, 1994.

14. Personal interview with Don Hicks, April 13, 1994.

15. Bob Woods, "Still Proving His Mettle," *Sports Illustrated,* Special Advertising Section, November 1992.

16. Telander, p. 50; personal interview with Rai Withers, April 19, 1994.

17. Shook and Greenwood, p. 33.

18. Personal interview with Rai Withers, April 19, 1994.

19. Woods, Nov. 1992

20. Personal interview with Rai Withers, April 19, 1994.

21. *Black Enterprise*, June 1990, June 1991, June 1992, June 1993. List of Top 100 Black-Owned Businesses.

22. Bishop, op. cit.; Dave Bing resume.

23. Personal interview with Rai Withers, April 19, 1994.

24. Bishop, op. cit.

25. Personal interview with Don Hicks, April 13, 1994.

26. Personal interview with Dave Bing, May 2, 1994.

27. Shook and Greenwood, p. 33.

Chapter 6

1. Personal interview with Juanita Bing, April 7, 1994.

2. Robert L. Shook and Ramon Greenwood, *The Name of the Game Is Life* (Chicago: Contemporary Books, 1992), p. 32.

3. Personal interview with Dave Bing, May 2, 1994.

4. Ibid.; personal interview with Don Hicks, April 27, 1994.

5. "Bing Saves School Sports," *Black Enterprise*, October 1989, p. 34.

6. "Charity Slam Dunk," *Fortune*, September 11, 1989, p. 210.

7. Ibid.

8. *Black Enterprise*, p. 34

9. Personal interview with Dave Bing, May 2, 1994.

10. Ibid.

11. Ibid.

12. Ibid.

13. Ibid.

14. Ibid.; "Arents Pioneer Medal Winners," *Syracuse Magazine*, Spring 1994, p. 50.

15. Fax from Dave Bing's office to EPS; *Syracuse Magazine*, p. 50.

Chapter 7

1. Rick Telander, "Life Lessons from a Man of Steel," *Sports Illustrated*, August 19, 1991, pp. 40, 49.

2. Ibid., p. 51; personal interview with Frank Nicoletti, April 27, 1994.

3. Personal interview with Dave Bing, May 2, 1994.

4. Telander, p. 51.

5. Personal interview with Dave Bing, May 2, 1994.

6. Personal interview with Earl Lloyd, April 7, 1994.

7. Personal interview with Don Hicks, April 13, 1994.

8. Personal interview with Morris Moorawnick, May 13, 1994.

9. Personal interview with Don Hicks, April 13, 1994; personal interview with William Rountree, April 8, 1994.

10. Robert L. Shook and Ramon Greenwood, *The Name of the Game Is Life* (Chicago: Contemporary Books, 1992), p. 29; (Remark by Sue Ray, Dave Bing's secretary to EPS); Mark Whicker, "Pistons' Man of Steals Shows Business Mettle," *Chicago Tribune*, June 17, 1988.

11. "Arents Pioneer Medal Winners," *Syracuse Magazine*, Spring 1994, p. 50.

12. Personal interview with Dave Bing, May 2, 1994.

13. Personal interview with Rai Withers, April 19, 1994; Bob Woods, "Still Proving His Mettle," *Sports Illustrated*, Special Advertising Section, January 1992.

14. Personal interview with Rai Withers, April 19, 1994.

GLOSSARY

All-Star players—Outstanding players in the game of baseball who are selected from among all of the teams in the league. An all-star game is played between two teams made up of the best players in the league.

assist—A pass that enables a teammate to score.

Basketball Hall of Fame—A building in Springfield, Massachusetts where basketball fans can go. The building houses exhibits and displays honoring outstanding basketball players throughout the history of the game.

draft picks—A system used by many professional sports for obtaining new players. The team that gets to pick a player first is usually a team that performed poorly the season before.

freshman—A college student in his or her first year of college.

Little League—An international baseball group for children. It was started in 1939. It originally included only boys between the ages of eight and twelve. Girls were included beginning in 1974. There are now two teen groups, one for ages thirteen to fifteen, and one for ages sixteen to eighteen.

morals—A set of standards having to do with right and wrong behavior.

Most Valuable Player—A player chosen by each individual team for helping the team in its effort to win games.

National Basketball Association (NBA)—A professional basketball league formed in the United States in 1949. The two top ranking teams at the end of each season play each other to see who will be NBA champion.

National College Athletic Association (NCAA)—A group founded in the United States in 1906. It makes the rules that college sports must follow.

Reserve Officers Training Corps. (ROTC)—A part-time training program for members of the military. It trains students in schools, colleges, and universities to become officers in the United States armed services. It tries to develop students for positions of military leadership during national emergencies.

Rookie of the Year—A new player chosen by the NBA as being the best new talent in the game.

scholarships—Awards of money to help pay for college.

sophomore—A college student in his or her second year of school.

starting lineup—Those players who are out on the basketball court when the game begins. They may be replaced later in the game.

varsity team—The main team representing a university, college, or school in sports competitions.

FURTHER READING

Allen, Mel R. "Going to See Dave." *Syracuse Magazine*, Spring 1994, 18-23.

Ashe, Arthur R., Jr. *A Hard Road to Glory, Basketball: The African-American Athlete in Basketball.* New York: Amistad, 1993.

"Charity Slam Dunk." *Fortune*, (September 11, 1989), 210.

Henderson, Tom. "Dave Bing's Best Turnaround." *Corporate Detroit Magazine*, (October 1991), 37-40.

"The Pistons' Bing." *Newsweek*, (January 8, 1968), 68.

"Power for the Pistons." *Time*, (February 2, 1968), 45.

Shook, Robert L. and Ramon Greenwood. *The Name of the Game Is Life.* Chicago: Contemporary Books, 1992.

Telander, Rick. "Life Lessons from a Man of Steel." *Sports Illustrated*, (August 19, 1991).

INDEX

ABOUT THE AUTHOR

Elizabeth Schleichert has been a self-employed writer since 1987. She and her husband have one son. When she is not writing she enjoys hiking, jogging, and gardening.